The Music of Nature

The Sayings of
ZHUANG
ZI

Edited and illustrated by

Tsai Chih Chung

Translated by

Goh Beng Choo

ASIAPAC • SINGAPORE

Publisher
ASIAPAC BOOKS & EDUCATIONAL AIDS (S) PTE LTD
2 Leng Kee Road
#02-08 Thye Hong Centre
Sinagpore 0315
Tel: 4751777, 4751773
Fax: 4796366

First published 1989
Reprinted 1989, 1990, 1991

© Asiapac Books, 1989

ISBN 9971-985-40-3

Printed in Singapore by
Loi Printing Pte Ltd

About the Editor/Illustrator

Tsai Chih Chung was born in 1948 in the Chang Hwa County of Taiwan. He began drawing cartoon strips at the age 17 and worked as Art Director for Kuang Chi Programme Service in 1971. He founded the Far East Animation Production Company and the Dragon Cartoon Production Company in 1976, where he produced two cartoon films entitled *Old Master Q* and *Shao Lin Temple*.

Tsai Chih Chung first got his four-box comics published in newspapers and magazines in 1983. His funny comic characters such as the Drunken Swordsman, Fat Dragon, One-eyed Marshal and Bold Supersleuth have been serialized in newspapers in Singapore, Malaysia, Taiwan, Hong Kong, Japan, Europe and the United States.

He was voted one of the Ten Outstanding Young People of Taiwan in 1985 and was acclaimed by the media and the academic circle in Taiwan.

The comic book of *The Sayings of Zhuang Zi* was published in 1986 and marked a milestone in Tsai's career. Within two years, *Zhuang Zi* went into more than 70 reprints in Taiwan and 15 in Hong Kong and has to-date sold over 175,000 copies. There is also a Japanese translation of the book.

In 1987, Tsai Chih Chung published *The Sayings of Lao Zi*, *The Sayings of Confucius* and a few books based on Zen and mythology. Since then, he has published 26 titles, out of which 10 are about ancient thinkers and the rest are based on historical and literary classics. All these books topped the bestsellers' list at one time or another. He is the pioneer in the art of visualizing Chinese literature and philosophy by way of comics.

About the Translator

Goh Beng Choo, a Singaporean, received her B.A. degree in Arts & Social Sciences from the University of Singapore (now known as the National University of Singapore).

Goh Beng Choo is a bilingual journalist with The Straits Times. She is currently attached to the Bilingual Desk, Section Two of the papers, where she reports and reviews arts and literary events organized in Singapore, Hong Kong and Taiwan in English and Chinese languages.

In 1987, she worked as a freelance stringer for the now defunct New Nation, writing serialized bilingual stories taken from Chinese proverbs. She has translated into English several poems and short stories written by Chinese-language writer Yeng Pway Ngon and is the translator of the Chinese translation of Tan Kok Seng's novel 'Son of Singapore'.

Translator's Note

As a bilingual writer who is no stranger to Chinese culture, translating this popular book into the English language has been both a challenging and pleasurable task for me.

Challenging because this book is a bestseller and there is bound to be curiosity on my part to test out if an English translation might be popular too.

Pleasurable because it was an opportunity for me to revise my reading of the ancient philosophers' thoughts which I first studied years ago as a young student - and which I enjoyed tremendously.

As a mature person approaching middle age, some of Zhuang Zi's ways of viewing the human society conveyed through the stories have a profound effect on me. They provide me with a refreshing way of accepting life's disappointments without being cynical about them. Then again, other viewpoints presented by him may be outdated but they contain such elements of beauty and imagination that they make for interesting reading to anyone who cares to pick the book up. I hope the reader likes this translated version of 'The Sayings of Zhuang Zi' as much as I've enjoyed translating it.

Goh Beng Choo

Publisher's Note

As a publisher dedicated to the promotion of Chinese culture and literary works, we are pleased to present you the Asiapac Comic Series by famous cartoonist Tsai Chih Chung to enable you to understand the schools of thought of the great ancient Chinese sages Zhuang Zi, Confucius and Lao Zi.

We hope the first of this series, *The Sayings of Zhuang Zi*, will bring you many hours of entertainment and enlightenment on Zhuang Zi's nonconformist and often humorous views of life.

We feel honoured to have Tsai Chih Chung's permission to the translation rights to his bestselling comics and would also like to thank Goh Beng Choo for putting her best efforts in the translation of this series.

Other Titles in the Asiapac Comic Series:

The Sayings of Confucius

The Sayings of Lao Zi

Foreword

A Fascinating Way With the Sages
Why a Cartoon Book on Zhuang Zi

It was my childhood ambition to be a cartoonist by profession. Since I started drawing cartoons at the age of seventeen, I have always felt that cartoons are the most intimate and powerful tools for penetrating readership.

It is difficult for a Chinese classic, written in ancient Chinese classical script, to stir up interest in the ordinary reader, but not a book of cartoons adapted from a Chinese classic and presented in simple everyday language. It is able to arouse in the reader a sense of curiosity which prods him on to flip through the pages and read on or even become interested in reading the original text. For this reason, I have ventured into the adaptation of famous classics through the ages and the first one is Zhuang Zi.

Everyone knows more or less about 'Zhuang Zi', the book and the philosopher. But many students turn a blind eye to and have no understanding whatsoever of Zhuang Zi's thoughts. The reason being simply a fear of reading in the Chinese classical script.

This book enables the reader to understand the essence of Zhuang Zi's thoughts in half an hour. I hope he likes it and reads it seriously. More so, I hope it may become his key to the treasure house of Chinsese classics and put him on the fascinating way to sharing or debating the thoughts of the great sages.

Tsai Chih Chung

Contents

THE SAYINGS
OF
ZHUANG ZI

The Music of Nature

1

Zhuang Zi's name is Zhou and Zhuang is his surname. He lived in the state of Song of the Warring States period. It was an era in which the strong states devoured the weak, the majority overpowered the minority; a chaotic and pain-stricken era. The sufferings of the world were like a bottomless pit. Were the sages buried underground to be regarded as great-minded or small-minded personalities? Zhuang Zi wondered.

1

From then on, Zhuang Zi shifted his vision away from worldly matters...

and cast his sight on the boundless time and space.

2

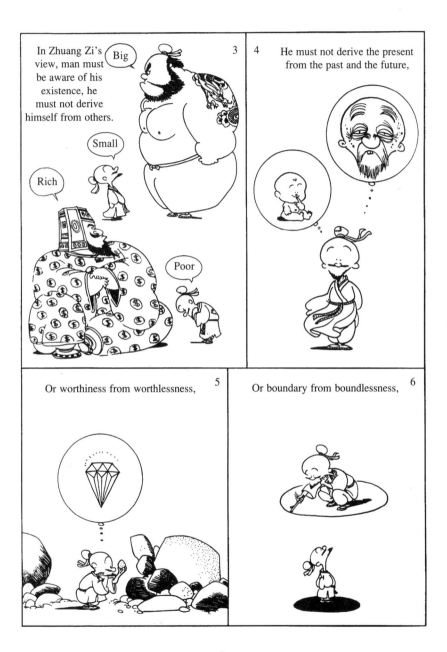

In Zhuang Zi's view, man must be aware of his existence, he must not derive himself from others.

Big

Small

Rich

Poor

3

4 He must not derive the present from the past and the future,

5 Or worthiness from worthlessness,

6 Or boundary from boundlessness,

7

Or life from death.
Only then can he gain freedom from restraints.

The philosophy of Zhuang Zi is a philosophy of
freedom. It is a philosophy by which life is
experienced in endless time
and space.

8

To him, the secular life is an
"order without life" whereas what
he set out to pursue is a
"life without order".

9

The Cicada
and the
'Ling' Turtle

It is said that Peng Zu lived for 800 years and was the longest-living man around.

1

But there is this little worm called Ephemera which is born at dawn and dead at dusk.

2

It has no idea how long a day is.

3

And there is this insect called Cicada, which is born in spring and dies in summer.

4

Yet there lived in the sea south of the state of Chu, a huge 'Ling' turtle in whose life span 500 years is but a spring and another 500 years an autumn.

It has no idea what the 'four seasons' are.

5

z
z

6

In prehistoric times, there was a tree named 'Chun', to which 8000 years was but a spring and another 8000 years an autumn.

The ephemera and the cicada can be called 'Small Year' while the 'Ling' turtle and the 'Chun' tree can be called 'Big Year'. The 'Small Year' will never understand the experience of the 'Big Year'.

Isn't Peng Zu just a 'Small Year' in comparison with the 'Ling' turtle and the 'Chun' tree?

I am 20 000 years old.

I am 12 000 years old.

I am 800 years old.

Isn't it sad for the 'Big Year' that people should regard Peng Zu as a case of longevity?

The Pride of the Little Sparrow

When the 'Peng'* flies, it soars up as high as 90 000 li**.

1

As for me, I would rather fly up to the tree top to sing.

Or down to the earth to catch the worms as freely as I can.

The flight, knowledge and vision of the little sparrow are different from that of 'Peng'.

4

Ha! Ha! Ha! Why does that fool bother to exert such great strength to fly so high?

2

3

We don't have to taunt the little sparrow nor envy the large 'Peng'.

5

* a legendary bird
** equivalent to 28 000 miles

7

The Large Gourds of Hui Shi

King Wei gave me some seeds of the large gourd.

1

3 But the quality of these gourds is so poor that when filled with water, they burst the minute I hold them up.

4 And when split in half, they are too shallow to hold much water.

I planted them and they grew big enough to hold five hectolitres of grain.

Hence the gourds may be big but they are quite useless. So I break them.

5

2

The Secret Formula of the Song Natives

A certain tribe of the state of Song excelled in making a kind of ointment.

1

When applied to the skin, the ointment prevented it from cracking.

2

3

For this reason, generations of the tribe had been engaged in the trade of bleaching cotton cloths.

One day a foreigner who heard about it came and acquired the secret formula for a hundred taels of gold.

4

What a treasure!

5

6

He offered the secret formula to King Wu and explained its usefulness in military affairs.

10

At that time, Wu and Yue were rival states. ⁷

When King Wu got hold of the secret formula, he started a river warfare during winter. ⁸

With the secret formula, troops of the Wu state were spared from catching chilblain* but the Yue soldiers who had no drugs to protect themselves suffered from skin disease and were defeated. ⁹

10 After the war, the man who offered the ointment was conferred with a large piece of land. He became a rich man and his status was elevated.

Though it was the same medical formula, those who did not know how to use it ended up bleaching cotton cloths for generations; while the man who used it in a creative way was rewarded with land and title.

* an inflammation sore, especially on the feet or hands, caused by exposure to cold.

11

5   Haven't you seen the fox and the wild cat?

In order to catch their prey, they leap and run with great agility...

6   Only to fall into a trap and die.

Whereas the yak has a huge body that hangs down like a cloud...

But it cannot catch a rat.

7

8

13

14

The Tattooed Natives of Yue

1 A native of Song loaded himself with hats and clothes to peddle in Southern Yue in the hope of making a big fortune.

2 Come, come, come and buy my beautiful clothes and fashionable hats!

3 But the natives of Yue cut their hair short, went about baring their tattooed bodies and wore no hats.

4 These clothes and hats are useless to us!

Whether an object is useful or whether a man is meritorious is all a relative matter which nobody ought to stick by rigidly. Whether Emperors Yao and Shun are meritorious and whether the Song natives' clothes and hats are useful are no absolute values.

15

6 The music of flute made by man comes either from the flute or the panpipe.

While the music of flute made by the earth is the 'sound of the wind'. The air that the earth emits is wind, and when the wind blows, all the holes and openings howl with it.

7

Some of the holes in the mountains and forests and trees are like human noses, mouths and ears, others are like circles and mortars, still others like deep pools and shallow pits.

The sound pouring out of these holes seems very much like storms, **8**

Or shooting arrows, squabbles or breath... **9**

10 It may be hoarse or fine, deep or urgent.

All the holes seem to respond in chorus... **11**

When the strong wind is over, all the holes are quiet again, with only the branches swaying... This is what I call 'Music of the Earth'... **12**

By itself the sound carries no feeling of anger, sadness, joy or happiness. These feeling are experienced when the human ear listens to the flute; they do not exist when one hears it as part of nature. Therefore feelings of anger, sadness, joy or happiness is man-made and not natural.

18

Zhao Wen Gives Up Playing Guzheng

1 Zhao Wen was a well-known musician who excelled in the playing of guzheng.

2 But he gave up playing the instrument in later years.

3 All because he had finally realized that when he struck a note to make music, the sound made by striking the other notes was lost...

4 Only when the instrument is not being played can the five notes of traditional Chinese music be preserved.

The principle behind man-made music and wood-carving is very much the same: When the final product takes shape, the other parts of the wood have been damaged and more is lost in the process.

The sound of nature is the only complete sound.

20

Is Xi Shi a Beauty?

If from the beginning, we had named heaven, 'Horse',

Horse
Horse

And earth, 'Finger',   2

Finger
Finger

3
Then heaven and earth would have been none other than 'Horse' and 'Finger'.

Horse
Finger

4 What man himself thinks is right is right and what he thinks is wrong is wrong. But what are the criteria for right and wrong?

5
To man, Xi Shi is a beauty, but to the fish, it may sink to the bottom of the water when it sees Xi Shi.

How beautiful!

How ugly!

When man creates knowledge from his viewpoint, he gets trapped by the self-designed 'Ring of Knowledge'.

22

The Tears of Lady Li

1 When Lady Li was to be married to Marquis Xian of the Jing state, she felt so sad that she cried and cried till her clothes were all wet.

I don't want to get married!

When she had, after some time, settled into the palace of Jing, slept in soft beds and tasted grand exotic feasts, she realized how silly it was to cry on the day of her wedding.

2

Everyone is afraid to die, but who knows if we are going to regret why we were ever born at all? Doesn't this bear some similarity to Lady Li's feelings before and after her wedding?

23

The Dream of the Recluse

1

The dreamer is often unaware that he is dreaming and consults the gods on his fate in the dream. He knows he is in a dream only when he wakes up.

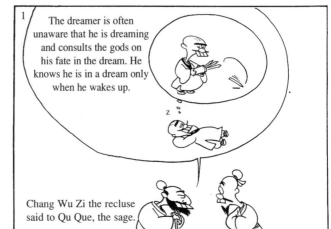

Chang Wu Zi the recluse said to Qu Que, the sage.

2

Only the enlightened man knows that life is a big dream, which some fools think they are enlightened.

3

You and I are dreaming. Even my claim that you are dreaming is dreamy talk.

You are dreaming!

Only those who are doubtful can be enlightened, the fools always think they are enlightened, which makes them fools in the final analysis.

24

Dialogue Between the Shadows

1

Wang Liang is the shadow of a shadow. One day, he called out to his master shadow...

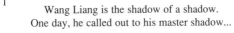

Hello!

2

You are always walking, stopping, sitting or standing, why?

3

That's because I have something to rely on. I can't help it.

4

The snake relies on its scales to slide, the cicada relies on its wings to fly.

5

But once they are dead, they wouldn't be able to fly or slide even with those scales and wings.

The law of nature is a law of change without a permanent ruler or permanent subjects. To be part of nature is to rely on nothingness.

25

Zhuang Zhou Dreams of a Butterfly

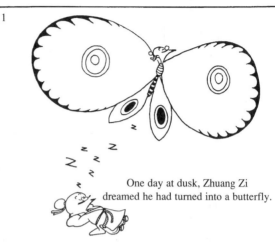

1

One day at dusk, Zhuang Zi dreamed he had turned into a butterfly.

2

Flapping his wings, he felt like a butterfly and was tremendously delighted.

At that moment, he forgot entirely that he was Zhuang Zi.

After a while, he came to realize that the gleeful butterfly was actually himself.

So was it Zhuang Zi who had changed into a butterfly in the dream or the other way round?

3

4

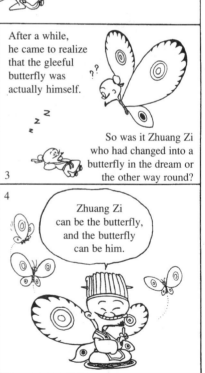

Zhuang Zi can be the butterfly, and the butterfly can be him.

Three in the Day and Four at Night

1

A monkey-keeper fed his monkeys with chestnuts.

2

He said to the monkeys one day:

Grr...

Suppose I give you three litres of chestnuts in the morning and four litres at night?

3

Then I shall give you four litres in the morning and three litres at night.

Yeh!

In reality three litres in the morning and four litres at night is no different from four in the morning and three litres at night. Yet it changed the mood of the monkeys. Do we humans make the same mistake as the monkeys? Think carefully.

Hui Shi Leans Against the Chinese Parasol

1

Hui Shi was known for his eloquence and had been engaged in debates for a great part of his life.

2

I've won!

I've lost!

Once, while resting against the tree, he came to the realization of the insignificance of debates.

Whenever he felt tired after a debate, he would lean against a Chinese parasol tree for a good rest.

And stopped bothering himself with the activity.

5

3

Do you really win by beating your opponents with eloquence? The very thought that you have succeeded makes you a failure.

30

The Fire Burns On

Tao!

Man's body may be dead one day,

Tao!

But his spirit,

Tao!

His ideas can be passed on from generation to generation.

Wood is burnt with oil and though oil may run out, fire continues to burn forever.

The conservation of life means not to conserve body but to conserve mind and spirit to keep it alive.

31

Pheasant in the Cage

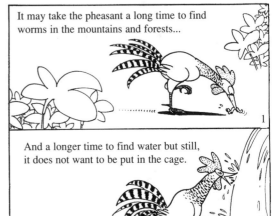

It may take the pheasant a long time to find worms in the mountains and forests...

1

And a longer time to find water but still, it does not want to be put in the cage.

2

That is because the bird may be well preened and fed in the cage,

But it does not have the freedom it enjoys in the open.

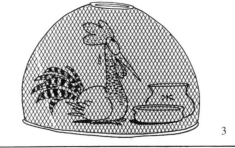

3

A man who knows the way of conserving life will not trade freedom for materialistic pleasures. But in real life, how many people enjoy the view of a clear blue sky above their heads?

33

The Horse-Lover

Once upon a time there was a horse-lover.

1

2 He attended to his horse with utmost care,

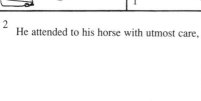

Using a bamboo basket to hold the droppings of the animal...

3 Once he used his hand to hit the blood-sucking flies on the horse's back...

4

Alarmed, the horse kicked him to death.

And a large sea-shell to hold its urine.

You may like someone but that person may not understand your love for him.

The Earth God's Tree

1 A master carpenter and his apprentices travelled to the state of Qi to build houses...

On the way, they came across a giant tree by a temple built in honour of the Earth God, whose top nearly touched the clouds.

3 I can't be bothered!

4 Master!

5 We have not seen such a huge tree since the day we became your apprentice, why don't you stop to take a look?

6 Forget it! That is merely a useless tree.

37

The Life Span of Trees

1

The Ling Shi district in the state of Song was ideal for growing catalpas, cedars and mulberry trees. The minute these trees grew as thick as a fist's girth, they were cut off to make posts for keeping monkeys.

2

Those trees which grew thicker were cut off to build tall houses.

3

While the thickest of them all were made into coffins for the rich.

4

As such these tree could never enjoy natural longevity, and died one after another in middle age.

What a pity! Those poor useful trees.

During ancient rituals when the wizards offered sacrifices to the River God, cows with white patches on the forehead, pigs with high snouts and men inflicted with piles would never be thrown into the river as sacrificial offerings because they were considered 'inauspicious'.

Some sagacious, adaptable personalities present themselves as 'inauspicious' and 'incompetent' men to protect themselves from disasters of the world.

6

The beautiful and the ugly have their unique qualities. There is no need to distinguish between the 'good' and the 'bad', the 'auspicious' and the 'inauspicious'.

Because of her good looks, the beauty became a sacrificial object for the River God. Is 'beauty' something 'auspicous' or 'inauspicious'?

The Incredible Eccentric

There was an eccentic who was born with a head bent below his navel, shoulder higher than the head and hair spiked. His five organs were askew and his loins sandwiched in between his thighs. This man's name was Zhi Li Shu.

1

He could support himself by just washing and mending clothes for people.

2

What he made from fortune-telling was enough to feed a dozen mouths.

3

When young men everywhere were enlisted into the army during wartime, he wandered about in the streets in big strides and was left alone very much.

4

When government officials were handing out welfare aids for the poor, Zhi Li Shu qualified as a recipient and received a great deal of firewood and rice.

5

A wise man is not bothered by physical handicap and ugliness. Handicap and ugliness may spare one from disasters.

The Oil Burns Itself Out

1
The tree is chopped off to make a handle for the axe, which is used to chop a tree in return.

2
The oil is used to light a fire, and ends up burning itself out.

The cinnamon tree is edible. It is chopped off and eaten by man.

Mmmm! Delicious!

3

The varnish tree is used in rust-proofing, its skin gets scraped off.

4

Most people in this world know the advantage of being useful: few know the advantage of being useless.

5

Historical figures such as Shang Yang, Wu Chi, Su Qin and Zhang Yi were intelligent men, but they all died a terrible death. 'Intelligence' can sometimes be the weapon that kills oneself.

41

The Tiger-Keeper

1 Keeping tigers is a dangerous hobby. The expert tiger-keeper never feeds it with a live animal.

2 It's because when the tiger is struggling with its prey, it is highly provoked.

3 With its aggressive instincts let loose, the consequences can be terrible.

That's why a tiger-keeper must be sensitive to the animal's temperament in order to control it.

4

Tigers too have their temperament and if you follow these inclinations, the animal wouldn't be ferocious and frightening after all.

With that sensitivity, tigers can be as tame as cats.

Meow!

Meow!

5

Toeless Shu Shan

In the state of Lu, there lived a man without toes. Everybody called him Teoless Shu Shan.

1

One day, he walked all the way on his heels to meet Confucius.

2

3 You had your toes cut off by the court officials because of misconduct. Its's too late for you to come and see me now.

I may have had my toes cut off, but I have more valuable features than toes, and the reason I have come to see you is to preserve these valuable features.

4

I'm terribly sorry!

Please come in to guide my disciples!

5

Because Toeless Shu Shan is a man of virtue, Confucius could not ignore him. Physical handicap alone does not incapacitate a man.

6 Without a word, Toeless Shu Shan turned around and walked out on him.

43

**Nature
Is
Just Like
Hercules**

Nature is just like Hercules, it operates with endless power.

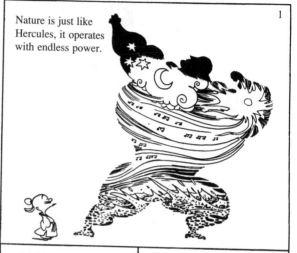

1

Nature gave me a body.

2

It labours me to sustain my livelihood.

3

It settles me into a secure old age with time.

4

It gives me eternal rest by death.

5

Nature is changeable and if man conforms to these changes, he can break free from joy and fear and see no difference between life and death.

Tao Is Forgotten

1 Zi Gong asked Confucius: Master, why do you travel around the state to have yourself bound by the practice of rites and education?

2 We can retreat from the world temporarily! But how?

A fish is in its element in the water.

A man is in his element with the practice of Tao.

3

4

5 The fish swims freely in the river, forgetting that it lives in water. We fish live in water.

Living in nature, the man who engages himself in Tao is so happy and contented that he often forgets about the existence of Tao.

7 Man lives with Tao.

A man is not his element when his heart is filled with all kinds of knowledge that are in compartments. It is important to penetrate knowledge and go beyond it.

6 Water? Where is it?

8 Tao? Where is Tao?

Zi Sang's Song of Poverty

1. Zi Yu and Zi Sang were close friends.

2. One day after it had been raining for months, Zi Yu dropped in on Zi Sang to give some rice.

3. Oh my father! Oh my mother! Heaven! Man!

What happened?

4. I am sick. For days I have been thinking...

5. Who made me so poor? Was it my parents? Was it heaven and earth?

6. My parents have nothing against me. Neither do heaven and earth. My poverty must be fated.

What is beyond man is called fate. Were you born a prince? A beggar? This is beyond your choice. Man must accept fate and live in harmony with Tao.

Are the Duck's Legs Too Short

What is long by nature will not be too long. Likewise, what is short naturally will not be too short.

1

A duck's legs may look terribly short yet you can't lengthen them. Once you do, the duck suffers.

A crane's legs may look terribly long but you can't cut them. Once you do, the crane suffers.

4

All because the short-legged duck has a long neck.

2

3

5

Isn't that convenient?

The long-legged crane has a short neck, and one complements the other.

6

Do not measure length by standards set by man. Do pay more attention to the natural usage and you will find what's long isn't too long and what's short isn't too short.

There is Tao in Robbers

51

The Fine Wine of Zhao State

1 The king of Chu once threw a banquet for the kings and lords from all the states, and the states of Lu and Zhao offered their best wine.

The wine from Zhao tastes good, can I have some?

No!

Your Highness, Zhao state sent us bad wine on purpose!

What a despicable act!

2

Despicable!

The wine officer got angry and he switched the wine from Lu and Zhao around.

3

4

When the king of Chu returned to his state, he immediately besieged Han Dun, the capital of Zhao.

Although good wine can please men, it too can create disasters.

5

wine

Nature's Companion

1. The essence of the perfect man who follows the wisdom of nature can be likened to the relationship between the body and its shadow...

2. And the relationship between sound and echo, in which questions are answered and feelings are reacted to.

3. Because his body and nature are one, when he stops he makes no noise.

4. When he moves he leaves no trails. Hence he is able to bring the confused world back to the great Tao.

5. Those who believe in the existence of the self are gentlemen who live from the Three Dynasties onwards. Only those who don't are nature's companions.

Selflessness is in harmony with nature's Tao. Man's body is only one of the many changes of nature. If you try to possess it, then your interest is purely selfish and personal.

The Old Man Who Makes Wheels

1. Once, while Duke Huan was reading in the hall, wheel-maker Pian was making wheels in the court.

2. May I know what book you are reading?

   I'm reading the great words of a sage.

3. Is the sage still alive?

   No, he is gone.

4. Then what you are reading is but a dross left behind by the dead.

5. What are you talking about? Tell me your reason, otherwise I shall order your death!

   Please don't be angry, Your Highness.

6. I am a wheel-maker, and I shall use wheel-making as an allegory to explain my view.

7. When I am shaping the wheel and going fast with the chisel, I save on strength but the wheel is not round. When I am slow I use more strength, but the wheel is round.

The best skill in wheel-making is not to be fast nor slow but to operate with just the right feel of strength.

8

But I have not been able to pass this skill to my son, which explains why I am still making wheel at 70.

9

It follows that the wisdom attained by the sage cannot be passed down to us. Therefore, aren't the books you are reading dross from the dead?

10

The artisan can only teach you the basic rules, not his success secret; the swordsman can only teach you the basic styles, not his skills. The intellectuals always value words printed in books, not knowing what's said in between the lines are more valuable. That explains why people who memorise passages are not necessarily good readers.

**Sky
and
Earth,
Sun
and
Moon**

Is the sky moving?

Is the earth motionless?

Do the sun and moon
take turns to shine?
What controls the sky
and the earth? The sun
and the moon?

Are clouds for
making rain?
Or is it the other
way round?

Everything
is nature.

57

The Seagull
and
the Crow

1. Confucius called upon Lao Zi to discuss benevolence and righteousness.

2. The whiteness of the seagull is not the result of daily baths.

3. The blackness of the crow is not the result of daily dyeing.

INK

4. Black and white are natural qualities, you can't say one is beautiful and the other is not.

White is beautiful!

Black is beautiful!

Nonsense!

5. You distinguish good and evil by the concept of benevolence and righteousness. To a man well-versed in the great Tao, you make the same mistake as the crow and the seagull.

Confucius Sees the Dragon

After meeting Lao Zi, Confucius remained silent for three days.

1

2

Master, what did you teach Lao Zi at your meeting with him?

Sigh... Sigh...!

3

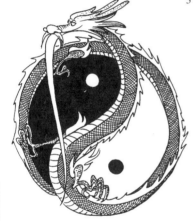

I saw the dragon. It followed the course of Yin and Yang and never ceased to change. I was dumbfounded with awe, how could I teach him anything at all?

To Confucius, Lao Zi has attained the Tao of nature and has an endless capacity for change. Words are redundant when one is faced with a man of Tao.

59

Don't Pierce the Ox's Nose

The Yellow River God asked the North Sea God: **1**

What is nature? What is the doing of man?

2

The ox and the horse each has four legs. This is nature.

The horse is bridled. **3**

4 The reins pierce through the nose of the ox. These are doings of man.

Any artificial knowledge, ethics and law is against nature, and is similar to piercing the ox's nose and bridling the horse.

Wind and Snake

Nao is a one-legged creature while Xian* has a hundred legs.

1

2

It is so convenient for me to walk on one leg. How do you manage with so many?

I slide on with nature's device for me. It comes easy.

3

!

4

5

I move with many legs, but I still lag behind you who has no legs. Why?

I operate according to nature's way. I don't need legs.

6 7

* a centipede-like creature

61

Courage of the Sage

1

When Confucius arrived at the Kuang district of Wei State, the residents there mistook him for a villain named Yang Hu and began to besiege him.

2

Do not panic, please stay on to listen to my preaching.

3

Why aren't you afraid, master?

Let me tell you, Zhong You.

4

It is the courage of the fishman not to fear the flood dragon*.

* a mythical storm-raising creature

63

The Frog in the Well

Learning to Walk the Handan Way

A boy from the Yan state set out to Handan, the state of Zhao's capital, to learn the way inhabitants of Handan walk.

1

2

Unfortunately, not only did he fail to pick up the typical Handanian's gait, he even forgot his own way of walking.

3

4

Oh dear, I don't know how to walk now!

5

He had no choice but to crawl home.

Initially, man reads to pursue the great Tao and resume his original nature. But after a long time, he gets lost in the city of books and can't come out of it,

The Owl Eats the Rotten Rat

1

Hui Zi was made Prime Minister by King Hui of Liang and Zhuang Zi decided to pay him a visit.

2

Zhuang Zi is here on the pretext of a courtesy call, he is actually after your position.

!

3

What's your motive in visiting me?

4

The legendary bird Wan Chu lives in the south and when it flies from the south to the north, it never rests on any tree other than the Chinese parasol,

The Joy of Fish

Zhuang Zi Dreams of the Skeleton

1 Zhuang Zi saw a skeleton on his way to the state of Chu.

72

The Sea-Bird Does Not Like Music

1

Yuan Ju is a gigantic sea-bird with a head measuring eight feet long. It has beautiful plumage and looks like a phoenix.

Yuan Ju has landed on the outskirt of the city!

Send someone to bring it to our imperial ancestral temple.

To welcome it, we must play the ancestral music...

And feed it with the best wine and food.

2

This is the best music of our state, isn't it beautiful?

3

4

75

The Drunkard Falls Off the Cart

1 A drunkard fell off his cart and was badly hurt but not dead.

Wine

2

Wine

3 Boy!

Wine

4 Because at that moment he was unaware that he was sitting in a cart and had fallen off it...

Wine

5 The fear of injuries or death had no place in his heart, therefore he wouldn't die.

Hey! Wait for me!

Wine

A drunkard is like a man who forgets his self-existence. The self-forgotten man is protected by nature.

76

On Clouds of Tao

77

80

81

The Swallow Nestles On the Eaves

1
What a wise bird the swallow is! Where it sees as unsafe, it does not go.

2
When the fruit it carries drops, it leaves it there.

3
Originally it was afraid of man but when it finally nestles on the eaves it is left alone.

4
This has relevance for man's way of dealing with life.

Birds are afraid of man and so nestles among mountains and high trees. The swallow is quite different, it lives on the eaves. One wonders what secret it has in avoiding trouble?

Geng Sang Chu Evades Fame

1

Geng Sang Chu, one of Lao Zi's disciples, had quite successfully attained the Tao of Lao Zi.

2

Geng Sang Chu lived in the Wei Lei Mountain, and the mountain people enjoyed good harvests and so, they began to feel grateful to him and worshipped him. When Geng Sang Chu heard about it, he said to his disciples:

3

In spring, the grass grows.

4

In autumn, everything bears fruit. These are nature's doings. But because I live here, the people credit me with what nature has bestowed on them and regard me as a sage. I wouldn't want to be their model.

5

So he moved to the forest.

88

Yellow Emperor Asks the Shepherd for Directions

Yellow Emperor and six sages - among them Fang Ming, Chang Yu, Zhang Ruo and Guo Ji - were riding on a chariot heading for Ju Ci Mountain to visit Da Kui. 1

The seven sages lost their way. 2

3

Do you know where the Ju Ci Mountain is?

Yes, I do.

4

Do you know where Da Kui is?

5

Yes, I do.

91

92

The Two States on the Snail's Feelers

1 King Hui of the state of Wei entered into an alliance with King Wei of the state of Qi. Soon after that, the King of Qi broke the alignment and enraged the King of Wei.

Attack the Qi State immediately!

2 Your Highness, please listen to me... You know of a small animal called the snail, don't you?

Yes, I do.

3 A man named Chu built a state on the left feeler of a snail, and another named Man built a state on its right feeler. The two states are always engaged in battles to fight over lands, in which tens of thousands of people are injured or killed.

4 Nonsense! How can that happen?

Your Highness, is there any boundary to the world?

5 No, there isn't.

6

7 In the centre of the world, there is a Wei State. Inside the Wei State, there is a Da Liang city.

In the city, there is a palace which houses a king. Is there any difference between the king and the States of Man and Chu?

In the eyes of the man of Tao, those worldly people who compete for lands and benefits are just like the two states fighting on the feelers of the snail.

93

94

The Prophetic White Tortoise

95

96

Natural Use

Zhuang Zi was giving Hui Zi quite a mouthful of lessons. 1

What you have said is useless! 2

Nonsense!

I can only talk to you about 'use' when you know what being useless means. 3

Take the earth for example. What you are using is only that tiny space on which you are standing. 4

If you dig away all the space outside your foothold... 5

Ah! 6

Would that foothold still be useful to you? 7

And so usefulness is founded on uselessness. There will be no usefulness without uselessness.

97

Forgetting the Bamboo Trap After the Catch

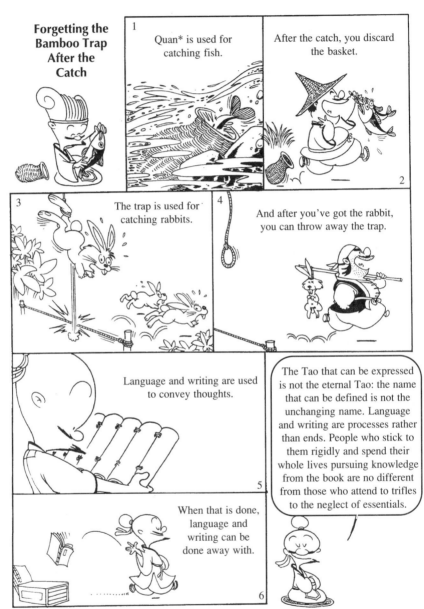

Quan* is used for catching fish.

After the catch, you discard the basket.

The trap is used for catching rabbits.

And after you've got the rabbit, you can throw away the trap.

Language and writing are used to convey thoughts.

The Tao that can be expressed is not the eternal Tao: the name that can be defined is not the unchanging name. Language and writing are processes rather than ends. People who stick to them rigidly and spend their whole lives pursuing knowledge from the book are no different from those who attend to trifles to the neglect of essentials.

When that is done, language and writing can be done away with.

* A bamboo basket

Yang Zhu Learns the Great Tao

Yang Zhu wanted to learn Tao from Lao Zi.

Master, can you please come and stay with me in the inn and teach me Tao?

1

You are hopeless! Your domineering attitude puts people off!

2

3 How can you ever cultivate Tao?

I shall listen to your advice!

4 When he first came to stay in the inn, all were terrified of him and none dared to sit at the same table with him.

5 But at the time when he was about to leave the inn, his attitude had changed a great deal. People were on such intimate terms with him that some of them even dared to snatch his seat.

Go away!

A man who wants to cultivate Tao must get rid of his arrogance first. How can one accommodate Tao when one's heart is filled with complacence?

99

Zi Gong's Snow-White Clothes

1

Yuan Xian and Zi Gong were students of Confucius.

2

Yuan Xian was so poor that the roof of his house often leaked.

3

And there were holes in the door, but he didn't seem to mind one bit.

4

Zi Gong had the gift of the gab and became a high official, moving about with airs. He decided to visit Yuan Xian one day.

5

The lane is too narrow, the carriage can't get in.

101

The Great Argument of a Robber

Liu Xia Ji was a friend of Confucius. He had a brother named Zhi who was a robber. Zhi led a band of 9,000 men who went around ravaging the states, robbing and killing people.

1

Parents ought to discipline their children and elder brothers ought to discipline their younger brothers. Now your brother has become a robber and goes around killing people. Can't you try and control him a little?

2

But some people just wouldn't listen to their elders, and there is nothing you can do.

3

4

Let me go and offer my exhortations to him.

That brother of mine is a tough guy, and if you go against his wishes, he will be furious. I think you'd better not try to advise him.

5

103

106

The Three Swords of Zhuang Zi

1
King Wen of Zhao State had a penchant for sword-play. Swordsmen from everywhere flocked to Zhao and as a result, more than 3 000 of them were gathered in the court.

2
Day and night, they engaged in one duel after another at the order of the king and in the three years, a great number of them were dead. But it failed to deter the king from pursuing the hobby.

3
Knowing of the king's obsession with sword-play, the feudal lords intended to revolt and seize the land of Zhao.

4
The prince became worried when he got wind of the conspiracy.

5
There is only one man who can stop the king from carrying on with sword-play.

Who?

Zhuang Zi.

7
I heard you are distressed over the king's indulgence in sword-play.

I am indeed.

* about 1 500 feet

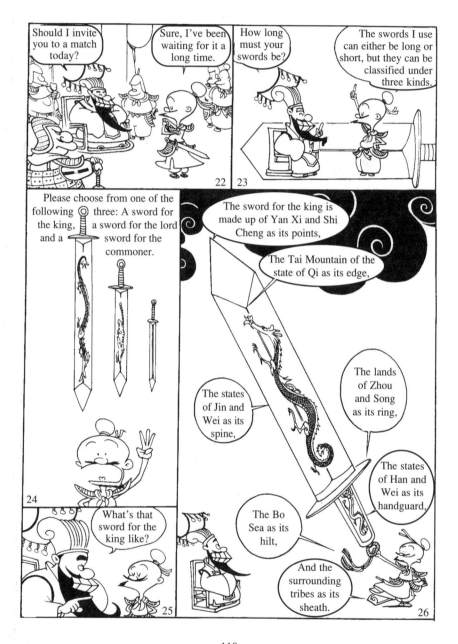

110

111

Confucius' Outing in the Black Forest

To do something you ought not to do is called '**meddling**'. Rambling on despite having your suggestion rejected is called '**wheedling**', figuring out people's minds and pleasing them with sweet words is called '**fawning**', agreeing with others without judgement is called '**toading**', criticizing people's weakness behind their backs is called '**back-biting**', breaking up friendship between two persons is called '**trouble-making**', praising the vicious while ostracizing people we detest is called '**intriguing**', and not telling good from evil while being ingratiating is called '**slippery**'.

Outwardly, these eight weaknesses create trouble for people; inwardly, they can damage the true self. They are qualities which a man of wisdom keeps clear of.

14

A penchant for taking on big jobs to seek credit and fame is called '**ambitious**', being self-righteous and self-important is called '**presumptuous**', defending one's faults while resenting exhortation from others is called '**stubbornness**', and finally, endorsing those with the same views as ours and condemning those with different views from ours is called '**bigotry**'.

What are the four shortcomings then?

15

16

It's difficult for us to discuss the goodness of the Great Tao with a man who is troubled by these four shortcomings.

17

To cultivate the Great Tao, one must not fall prey to the eight weaknesses and four shortcomings. They are the most common faults of men of the world.

Confucius' face changed colour when he heard this.

18

The
Man
Who
Hates
His
Footprints

The Man Who Hates His Shadow

1 There was a man who hated his shadow.

2 Go away, I hate you!

3

He began to walk faster and faster when he saw his shadow hot on his heels.

But when he hurried, his shadow hurried along too.

He started to run till he finally...

...dropped dead.

The behaviour of a man who doesn't understand the great Tao resembles that of the shadow-hater. It's actually quite simple to get rid of shadows: Just take a rest in the shade and the shadow will disappear. Men of this world are all running not resting. Why is that so?

The Wandering Unmoored Boat

The skilled labours.

The intelligent worries.

The incompetent seeks nothing and wanders around when his stomach is filled.

Like a boat which breaks free from the rope and sways gently on the water.

Intelligence and skills often bring endless burden, which men of this world are often unaware of.

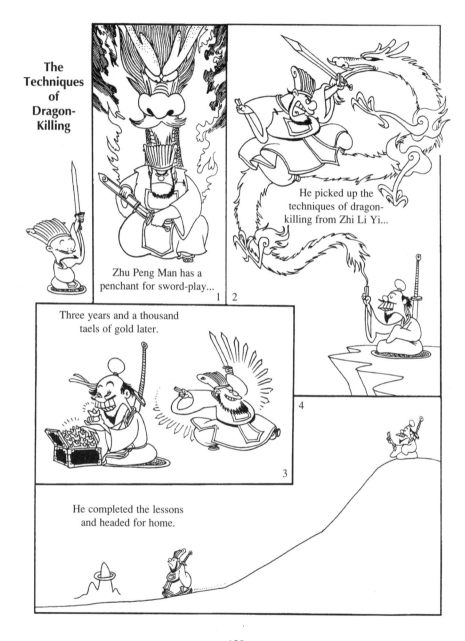

The Techniques of Dragon-Killing

Zhu Peng Man has a penchant for sword-play...

He picked up the techniques of dragon-killing from Zhi Li Yi...

1
2

Three years and a thousand taels of gold later.

4

3

He completed the lessons and headed for home.

121

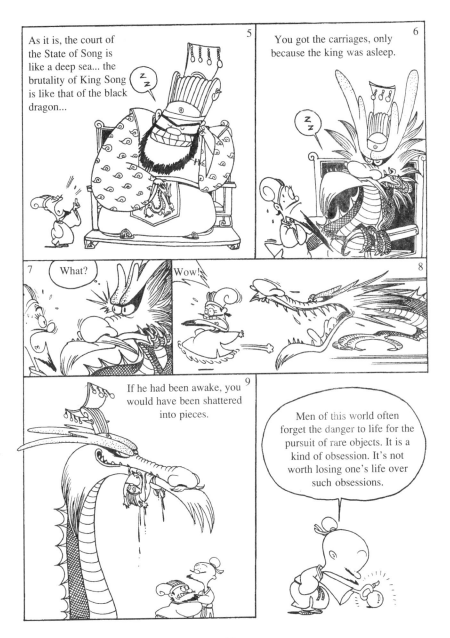

123

Zhuang Zi Is Dying

1 At Zhuang Zi's deathbed, his disciples gathered round to plan an elaborate funeral for him.

2 Why bother? When I'm dead, I shall have heaven and earth as my coffin, sun and moon as my ceremonial jade, stars as my pearl and all things under the sun as my gifts. Is there a better funeral ceremony than this?

3 But master, you will be eaten up by the crows and the hawks!

4 On the earth, I will be eaten up by the hawks. Underground, I will be eaten up by the cicadas and the ants. Why snatch the food away from the crows and the hawks to offer it to the cicadas and the ants?

Death is a natural phenomenon. The dissipation and changes of the human body are best left to nature to handle.

《亚太漫画系列》

自然的箫声

庄子说

编著：蔡志忠
翻译：吴明珠

亚太图书（新）有限公司出版